With the compliments of

THE GRAND BAHAMA DEVELOPMENT COMPANY LIMITED

GEORGE W. KATES
President

WILLIAM P. FISHER
Executive Vice-President

With thirty-four color plates

HANS W. HANNAU

FREEPORT/LUCAYA
GRAND BAHAMA ISLAND

Argos inc.
PUBLISHERS
Miami and Munich

Wrapper and cover designed by Gerhard M. Hotop

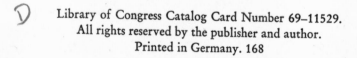
Library of Congress Catalog Card Number 69–11529.
All rights reserved by the publisher and author.
Printed in Germany. 168

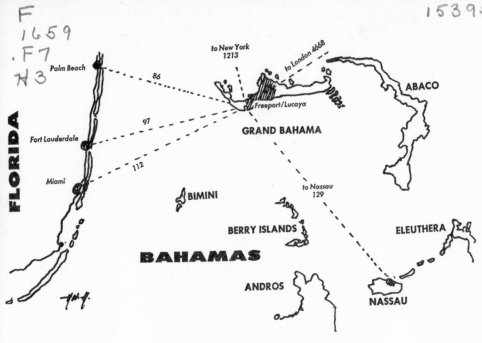

Within five years an unimportant, "undesirable" spot has become one of the happiest, busiest and most successful little towns in the Americas. First came business and business opportunities in and around Freeport and the harbor, then came a beautiful residential development, Lucaya. In the last few years thousands of young and old people have come from all over the world – Americans, English, Scandinavians, Canadians, Germans – the young to work under excellent conditions, the old to enjoy retirement in the climate of Paradise while investing their money in sound new projects. The population has doubled from year to year, to more than 21,000 residents in early

1968. New trades, enterprises, industries start almost every day, growing to the west. New residential sections develop in beauty and grace to the east, connected by well-planned, romantic waterways, separated by extensive golf courses with picturesque little lakes and ponds.

All this was envisioned about 1955 by the founder, Wallace Groves. Embryo of this small world was the idea of tax freedom connected with an industrial development, anchored in a long range contract with the Bahamas government. Thereby these wastelands were changed into an idyllic town. Wallace Groves is not only the founder, he is the developer and leader of this heady community, with the aid of a few dedicated, talented friends like Keith Gonsalves, Doug Silvera and others who believed in his dreams, ideas and ideals.

Freeport/Lucaya is today an internationally important trade center and harbor and a far-famed resort. Lucaya has become the fast growing, dreamed-of home town to many thousands of people. It will soon also be a center of international finance, education and science. And there is space, plenty of space, around the present community to extend and to grow for many, many years to come.

What is the meaning of "Lucaya"?

The word Lucaya comes from the name of the Indians who once populated the Bahamas. The Lucayan Indians whom Columbus found in the Bahama Islands when he made his first landfall on October 12, 1492, were "healthy, handsome and happy," he wrote. "This country excells all others as far as the day surpasses the night in splendour; the natives love their neighbours as themselves; their conversation is the sweetest imaginable; their faces always smiling; and so gentle and so affectionate are they, that I swear . . . there is not a better people in the world." Of the water around the islands he wrote, "The sea is so transparent, we could see it to the bottom. The tropical fish rivalled the beauty of the flowers."

Ponce de León made a landfall on Grand Bahama in 1513, searching for a fountain

6

on the island of Bimini which had, according to Lucayan legend, magical properties. The Spaniards responded to the generosity of the Lucayans by taking them for forced labor in the mines of Haiti, where they disappeared as a people entirely. So lacking in natural resources were the Bahamas that the Spaniards did not even bother to claim them. They were a sort of no-man's land until Charles I of Britain included them in a grant to Sir Robert Heath in 1627. Difficulties in Bermuda led Puritans from that island to the Bahamas in the 17th century, but because the soil was poor and pests destroyed the crops, few remained. Due to the lack of law and the fine strategic location beside the Gulf Stream, highway home to Spain for the Spanish plate fleets, piracy was the first enterprise to thrive among these islands. In 1726 Governor Woodes Rogers, the first Royal Governor, hanged many pirates and the Bahamas adopted its motto: "Expulsis Piratis Restituta Commercia."

To the Bahamas in the American Revolution fled many American Loyalists, bringing their slaves with them. Slavery was never economically important there, because potential for raising crops for export was negligible. Britain abolished the slave trade in 1807. Many Loyalists went back to England, many emigrated to the Florida keys – then a land beyond the law. The Royal Navy frequently seized foreign ships passing through those waters and freed the slaves-to-be. Britain freed the slaves on August 1, 1834. For some generations entire islands had only Negro inhabitants, banded together in small communities. One described that life: "We had too much fun. What I had was yours and what you had was mine. We grow pumpkins, cassavas, melons, sweet potatoes, cantaloupes, sugar cane and pigeon peas. We make a little money by making charcoal. And there were all the fish we wanted and we shared them."

Grand Bahama

Over the centuries Grand Bahama was a lonely island of rolling pineland and virgin beaches, all but uninhabited. What little history the Bahamas saw passed by this island, the fourth largest. It had no decent natural harbor. The pirates never bothered

7

with it, nor did the blockade runners who brought a brief boom to New Providence island in the Civil War, when they ran contraband past the Union fleet into southern ports. There was no recorded population until 1841. Grand Bahama lies 76 miles east of Palm Beach. It is about 80 miles long and averages 4½ to eight in width. A rocky ridge of oolitic limestone runs down the spine of the island, with elevations up to more than 70 feet above sea level. There are 60 miles of splendid coral sand beach along the south shore. The land slopes off on the flat north shore to tidal flats where bonefish abound. Pothole soils are good for vegetables and fruit. Some of the marl soil is good for pineapples, native to the West Indies. But mostly the level land was, until just yesterday, mantled with tall pine and scrub palmetto, fringed with magnificent sea grape trees near the shore.

Because Grand Bahama is the island closest to the United States, Prohibition in 1920 brought its first boom. Rum-runners congregated about the little village of West End, and it sometimes seemed that the western tip of the island might subside under the mountains of whiskey, rum, gin and Dutch beer awaiting transshipment to quiet coves and beaches of Florida in small, fast, shallow-draft boats. In 1933 this ended. Big-game fishermen prized it as a base for angling expeditions, but mostly the island slept in the sun.

Wallace Groves

The population of Grand Bahama in the official census of 1953 was 4,095, centered largely at West End and scattered through a few quaint villages the length of the island. Along about that time Wallace Groves, American financier-industrialist set up a lumber mill on the pine ridge, to timber the tall, hard-hearted virgin pines. Nobody is quite sure what he saw in the uninhabited pinelands in the center of the island. Maybe he noted how much it looks like South Florida, with the same infertile oolitic limestone, the same pines and palmettos, the same lack of a good natural harbor. Maybe he remarked that the climate was even more admirable than Florida's. Maybe he remembered what Henry Flagler said when he brought his railroad to Miami in 1896: "Miami will never be anything but a fishing village for the guests of my hotel." Maybe he was captivated by the unrivalled beaches and the clear water of the south shore. Whatever it was he was thinking about, Mr. Groves' eye lit on vast amounts of Crown lands about 25 miles from West End. There the island is bisected by a waterway, Hawksbill Creek, navigable by shallow-draft fishing boats. There he decided to build something.

The Hawksbill Creek Act

With representatives of the Crown and the Government of the Bahamas and with his attorneys, Wallace Groves sat down and the Hawksbill Creek Act resulted. The title reads: "An act to authorize the entering into an agreement with a company to be incorporated in the colony by Wallace Groves for the dredging of a deep water harbour and the establishment of an industrial area at and in the vicinity of Hawks-

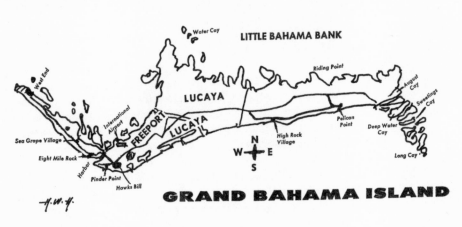

bill Creek, Grand Bahama." The agreement that resulted is between the Grand Bahama Port Authority, with Mr. Groves as president, and the Bahamas Government. This agreement, in effect, is a charter to free enterprise to build a microcosm.

Specifically, the Port Authority agreed, among other things, to dredge and construct a deep water harbor and turning basin at Hawksbill Creek and construct a wharf for cargo vessels within three years. This facility would be declared a private port, to be administered by the Port Authority. Under the agreement the Port Authority leased certain lands from the Crown and acquired others which came to about 51,500 acres in the vicinity of Hawksbill Creek. There was an option for an additional 50,000 acres. In this area the Port Authority agreed to establish schools, medical facilities, free living and office accommodations including electric current and other utilities for employees of the government, and facilities for the health, safety and sanitation of the Port Area and its population. The Port Authority agreed to use its best efforts to employ and train the Bahama-born wherever possible. In return, the Port Authority got numerous privileges, chief among them tax and import benefits and the assurance of freedom of operation.

As important to the residents who now live there as to the companies operating at Freeport/Lucaya are the tax benefits granted. Until 1990, there will be no real property taxes on lands or buildings within the Port Area. Until 1990, the Port Authority and its Licensees will be free from personal property taxes, capital gains taxes and capital appreciation taxes. Until 1990, the Authority and its Licensees will pay no taxes on earnings in the Port Area, and employees of same (provided they are ordinarily resident in the Freeport Area) will pay no taxes on their salaries or bonuses. Until 2054, the Port Authority and its Licensees will pay no import duties (except on goods for personal use or gifts). Until 2054, the Authority will pay no excise taxes (except on consumable goods imported into the Port Area), no export taxes and no stamp taxes on bank remittances.

As to licenses and freedom of operation, while the Bahamian Government remains responsible for the maintenance of law and order, the Port Authority, a private corporation, alone has the right to grant licenses to such firms or individuals who apply to it and to negotiate mutually satisfactory contracts. Subject to its obligations to ensure that provision is made for health, safety and sanitation, the Port Authority, together with its licensees, has the sole right to plan, lay out and vary the development of the Port Area. The licensees operate their businesses relatively free of Governmental restriction and subject only to agreements made between them and the Port Authority. Although the Port Authority is not to assign its rights to any person without consent of the Government, there is virtually nothing to prevent the Port Authority from licensing persons or carrying on any business, undertaking or enterprise within the Port Area.

What about the people who would man such potential enterprises? The Port Authority agreed to use its best efforts to employ Bahamians and to train them for better jobs, where possible, and to see that all licensees do the same. However, the Port Authority and its licensees have the right to import and employ key, trained or skilled personnel as well as unskilled labor that cannot be recruited by the government.

The Port Authority has since bought other land from private owners and now has control over an area of 233 square miles. Under supplemental agreements, made in 1960 and 1966, the Port Authority obligated itself to build a luxury hotel, to extend water and electrical service to certain communities outside the port area and to construct low cost homes. Other than a benign climate and magnificent beaches, almost the only thing the land itself contributed was an aquifer with a bountiful supply of fresh water.

Building a Small New World

The deep water port at Hawksbill Creek was built promptly by international investor D. K. Ludwig, under a license from the Port Authority, but for some years nothing much else seemed to happen. The only entertainment on Grand Bahama in 1960 was on Saturday night at the Risk Enterprise Ballroom or the Blue Marlin Tavern (a Holy-Roller church on Sunday morning.) One danced, and watched the people dance as one drank beer. People danced not as sublimation, not as a substitute for anything else, but for the love of the swaying and melodic rhythm itself. Then word got about and everything accelerated. The population of Grand Bahama in 1963 was 8,454. In 1967 Freeport/Lucaya was home to more than 17,000 residents from 17 nations, and Grand Bahama had a population of 35,250 people. More than 300,000 tourists visited the new resort in 1967. The new world a-building consists of two sections, Freeport and Lucaya. Freeport has been developed for industry and commerce within easy reach of the port, harbor and Freeport city center. It has one of the finest deep water harbors, with the largest oil bunkering installation, in the Western Hemisphere. Lucaya, the eastern 100,000 acres, has been reserved for homes and hotels, apartments, beach facilities, yacht havens, marinas, an exotic international shopping center and general recreational facilities which include two beautiful gaming casinos.

Freeport

At the end of 1967 the total investment in industry and commerce in Freeport was $ 500,000,000, thanks to the tax advantages and geographical location of the fine harbor. In 1967, 1,830 vessels called there. Tourism has been largely responsible for the fantastic growth of the last few years. But the 1,242 Freeport licensees in 1968 include a $ 50,000,000 cement mill built by a subsidiary of U. S. Steel, a chemical plant for the manufacture of pharmaceuticals by Syntex Corporation (one of the largest manufacturers of birth control pills) and plants for paint manufacture, tire retreading, soft drink bottling, printing, swimming pool construction and ice production. There are 8,162 telephones in service in 1968, and there is a direct telephone service to Florida. The jet airport has daily jet service by six airlines: Air Canada, Bahamas Airways, British Overseas Airways Corporation, Eastern, Northeast and PanAm. It is also a mecca for private planes on recreational flights from all parts of the world.

Lucaya

Development of residential, hotel, tourist and recreational facilities has become the responsibility of the Grand Bahama Development Company Limited. The company, a joint venture of the Grand Bahama Port Authority and certain Canadian and American financial interests, is headed by George W. Kates as president, one of the most dynamic leaders in Freeport/Lucaya. Under his guidance the dream of an idyllic resort-residential community is coming into being.

The Hotels

By the end of 1967 the hotels in the garden city resort offered 2,516 rooms and included luxurious resort hotels, fine in-town hotels and several excellent motels. The opening of the Lucayan Beach Hotel in 1964 started a spree of hotel building. Now the less formal Lucayan Harbour Inn and Marina have made this a vast complex for leisurely living. The largest Holiday Inn in the world, with 614 rooms, opened in October, 1965, with beachside daytime life and sumptuous elegance at night. The lively Oceanus opened in 1965, as did the King's Inn and Golf Club. King's Inn boasts the largest golf layout in the Caribbean, with two 18-hole, par- 72 championship courses, laid out by the late architect Dick Wilson of Delray Beach. At the same time the modern Freeport Inn opened in the center of the business district. The Sheraton Oceanus-South, with its 16 floors the highest building in the Bahamas, opened early in 1968. These are the hotels that host the social and business leaders of the western world when they come to Freeport/Lucaya, unless – as so many do – they have their own vacation homes there.

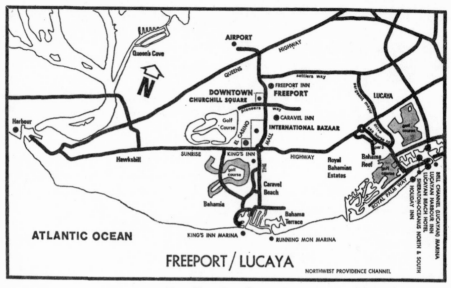

Downtown Freeport and Hotel Section of Lucaya

The Gaming

Lucayan Beach's Monte Carlo captures the sophistication and splendor of the grand old European gambling palaces. There the visitor can try his luck at black jack, craps, roulette, the slot machines. It is the first of the two casinos to be built under the legalized gambling permit. El Casino, the second, resembles a lavish Moorish palace. Its exotic golden dome is a landmark next to the International Bazaar, near downtown Freeport. There 3,000 guests never even jostled each other on opening night. There dinner-jacketed European croupiers man a vast array of gaming tables, and there clink row upon row of slot machines. Besides legalized gambling, the Kasbah at El Casino runs a continuous revue that is reminiscent of the best of Paris, Broadway and Las Vegas.

Night Clubs and Restaurants

Grand Bahama Island is a nightlife place. In entertainment you can sample it all, including native fire dancers, limbo and voodoo artists, famous names in show business, comedy combos and Latin American dancers. There are scores of places to enjoy, things to do. Fine restaurants galore offer a choice of cuisines – French, English, Italian, Polynesian, American, Bahamian and Oriental. No visitor should forget to sample conch salad, a native gourmet adventure.

International Bazaar

One can stroll around the world in Freeport's International Shopping Bazaar, enjoying an amazingly authentic duplication of the sights, sounds, smells, styles and people of some of the world's greatest cities. One can sample the atmosphere of such places as Tokyo's Ginza, Algiers' Casbah and Copenhagen's Frederiksberggade. The Bazaar is divided into sections – Arabian, Bahamian, French, Indian, Latin, Oriental, English, German and Scandinavian. One can shop for luxuries from all over the world. The food is as authentic as are the wares of the various areas, and the entertainment ranges from a belly dancer in El Khalife to a replica of the Danish village of Odensoe where Hans Christian Andersen lived and wrote.

The World of Water

With all the magnificent man-made attractions that have been conjured into being on the island, it is still the unexportable sun, sand and sea that are the basic charm of the resort. The coral sand beaches stretch for 60 miles. There are boats for hire. Water lovers can rent a speedy sailing catamaran for a few hours and explore hidden beaches, or try the new adventure of para-sailing (water skiing with a parachute). There is trolling, reef-fishing, surf-casting or drift fishing, with experienced guides and sound charter boats, and for all no license is required. Catches include blue and white marlin, sailfish, wahoo, tarpon, kingfish, grouper, mackerel, snapper, amberjack and scores of others. So clear and photogenic is the undersea world around the islands that the Bahama waters have been locations for numerous undersea motion pictures.

The resort is a suburb of paradise for the experienced Scuba diver and the novice snorkeler. There are plenty of great coral reefs near shore and plenty of equipment for rent and air for refill of tanks on shore. You don't have to be an intrepid diver to enjoy the undersea world, nor even a champion swimmer. Put on a float or life jacket, slip over the side of your boat, don face mask and snorkel and you can float for hours on the surface, rocking gently as do the lavender sea fans in the warm sea. What the undersea tourist looks for is coral patches, for these are the homes of hordes of jeweled tropical fish – the brilliant and comic parrot fish that graze on coral; angel fish, beau gregories, four eyed butterfly fish, yellow tail demoiselles and many more. All the colors are beautiful, all the movements graceful. Equipment and instructions by professionals are available. On Grand Bahama (Lucaya) is the international headquarters of the Underwater Explorers Society, with marine biology and color photo laboratories, research library, underwater museum, training pools, classrooms, a luxury gym and sauna in an attractive building at the gateway of the Oceanus-North hotel. If you want to see the underwater world without getting wet, there are glass-bottom boats.

>

Activities on the Beautiful Beach of Lucaya
Sport und Vergnügen am schönen Sandstrand von Lucaya
Actividades en la linda playa de Lucaya

Harbor at Lucayan Beach Hotel
Anlegestelle beim Lucayan Beach Hotel
Embarcadero del Lucaya Beach Hotel

El Casino

Lucayan Country Club
Lucaya Golfplatz und Klub
Lucaya campo de golf y casa club

Homes of Lucaya
Einfamilienhäuser in Lucaya
Casas Particulares en Lucaya

The Home of Wallace Groves
Das Heim von Wallace Groves
La residencia de Wallace Groves

Wallace Groves, Founder of Freeport/Lucaya, With his Family
Wallace Groves, der Gründer von Freeport/Lucaya, mit seiner Familie
Wallace Groves, el fundador de Freeport/Lucaya con su familia

The Beautiful Natural Beaches of Lucaya
Der herrliche Sandstrand von Lucaya
Las bellas playas naturales de Lucaya

Treasure of Lucaya
Der Schatz von Lucaya
El tesoro de Lucaya

Underwater Exploring in the Clear Ocean Around Lucaya
Entdeckungen unter Wasser im klaren Ozean von Lucaya
Exploracion submarina en las aguas claras de Lucaya

Hotels of Lucaya (View over Bell Channel Bay)
Die Hotels von Lucaya (Blick über die Bell Channel Bay)
Hoteles de Lucaya (Vista de la Bahia Bell Channel)

Freeport International Jet Airport
Der internationale Düsenflughafen in Freeport
El aeropuerto jet internacional en Freeport

Lucayan Marina, Bell Channel Bay
Bootshafen an Bell Channel Bay (Lucaya)
Marina de Lucaya en la Bahia Bell Channel

Fun around a Swimming Pool (Holiday Inn)
Leben und Treiben um das Schwimmbassin des Holiday Inn Hotels
Actividades alrededor de la piscina del Holiday Inn

Holiday Inn, Lucaya
Holiday Inn Hotel, Lucaya
Hotel Holiday Inn, Lucaya

Anglican Church of Freeport
Anglikanische Kirche in Freeport
Iglesia Anglicana

OUR SAVIOUR LUTHERAN CHURCH

The Famous Deep Water Harbor of Freeport
Der berühmte Tiefwasserhafen von Freeport
El famoso puerto de agua profundo en Freeport

In a Freeport School
In einer Schule Freeports
En una escuela de Freeport

Medical Center, Freeport
Ärztliche Zentrale in Freeport
Centro Medico de Freeport

A Beautiful Seascape of Lucaya
Am schönen Strand von Lucaya
Playa romantica de Lucaya

Oriental Building, Freeport
Orientalisches Gebäude in Freeport
Edificio oriental en Freeport

Tropical Park in the Heart of Freeport
Tropischer Park im Zentrum von Freeport
Jardin tropical en el corazon de Freeport

Hotel Oceanus-South, the Highest Building in the Bahamas Waterfall in the Middle of Town
Hotel Oceanus-South, das höchste Gebäude in den Bahamas Ein Wasserfall inmitten der Stadt
Oceanus Hotel-Sur, el edificio mas alto en todas las Bahamas Una cascada en el centro de la cuidad

Growing Lucaya – New Buildings, New Waterways, New Roads
Lucaya wächst: neue Gebäude, neue Wasserwege, neue Straßen
Lucaya crece: nuevos edificios, nuevas vias acuaticas, nuevas carreteras

Villas and Homes on the White Beaches of Lucaya
Villen und Familienhäuser entlang des weißen Strandes
Villas y residencias a la orilla de la playa blanca

London Double-Deck Buses for General Transportation
Londoner Doppeldeck-Autobusse für den allgemeinen Verkehr
Como en Londres, autobuses de dos pisos para el transporte publico

Kings Inn Country Club
Auf dem Golfplatz des Hotels Kings Inn
El campo de golf del Hotel Kings Inn

The Indian Section of the International Bazaar
Im indischen Teil des Internationalen Bazars
El sector Indio del Bazar Internacional

Kings Inn Country Club
Auf dem Golfplatz des Hotels Kings Inn
El campo de golf del Hotel Kings Inn

The Indian Section of the International Bazaar
Im indischen Teil des Internationalen Bazars
El sector Indio del Bazar Internacional

El Casino at Night
El Casino bei Nacht
El Casino de noche

Treasure Hunting

All this, and treasure, too . . . . It seemed almost too much when, in 1965, four like-able young men found several million dollars' worth of treasure in the form of silver coins minted about 350 years ago and bearing the insignia of Philip the Fourth of Spain. The young men, who own and operate the water skiing and skin diving school at the Lucayan Beach Hotel, reported that the find was made 1,000 yards offshore in about 20 feet of clear water. The treasure was discovered when Gary Simmons ducked under to look at what seemed to be a coral-encrusted ancient anchor. It was an anchor, all right, but it was encrusted with silver coins, mostly crude pieces-of-eight struck from flat bars of silver. There are reported to be at least three more treasure sites just offshore.

Land Sports

Sports-loving landlubbers can find their heart's desire in Lucaya, too. The golfer can play 72 holes of golf without repeating one hole, on fairways that are forever green. The Lucayan Country Club course, the two 18-hole courses of King's Inn and Golf Club, and the Bahama Reef Country Club course are all of championship calibre, well-trapped and expertly designed. The Seawind Club has a nine-hole par-three course lighted for night play. Throughout the resort are all-weather composition tennis courts, some lighted for night play and some with skilled professionals. For those who feel that the horse is man's best friend, there is nothing like a horseback ride down the beach.

The first annual International Grand Bahama Grand Prix of Formula Vee came to Grand Bahama in December, 1967, with ten days of fun and excitement, highlighted by a Junkanoo Parade with revelers filling the streets. The colorful celebration of Junkanoo, which can be traced back to old slave days in the West Indies, has been celebrated in the Bahamas for many years and remains one of the most exciting and interesting festival rites. Racing was programmed on the T-shaped 2.2 mile Freeport/ Lucaya course. The new circuit, one of the most beautiful race courses in the world of motor racing, winds along the Mall, past the Pub and King's Inn, around El Casino, and then, after a twisting bit of the Mall, finishes in front of the International Bazaar.

Skeet, trap and flyer shooting, bowling, billiards, Rugby, soccer, volleyball, badminton, table tennis are all popular sports in that sunny world.

Homes of Lucaya

It is not the treasure under the sea, nor the click of the roulette ball that by 1967 had brought citizens from all over the world to live in 1,701 homes and 2,619 apartments in Lucaya. Many fled grubbiness, grime and cold. Many were attracted by the adventure of being pioneers in a new city they could help mould. The effervescent city built from scratch in this decade has that indefinable charm that has made more than 21,000 people say, "I want to call this place home." The residential area is planned to have compactness without over-crowding, liveability everywhere and elegance where it is desired. Nowhere is industry cheek-by-jowl with homes. Yet everywhere the people who live and work there are no more than ten minutes from their jobs in Freeport. Lucaya is a city you can love, not a suburban sprawl. Architects, attorneys, physicians, bankers, accountants, scientists, motion picture makers, business employees and business leaders can choose homes in a wide price range. Attractive architecture with a Bahama flavor, modern public utilities and water, an excellent building code, many churches, modern schools, a fine hospital, Little League baseball teams and various service clubs are among the amenities of modern life that make residence here complete. Television and radio reception from the United States is good. People come to play, remain to live, launch businesses and work in Freeport. Their city is urban and urbane, traffic-jam free, with green recreation strips running between back gardens. And all this in a climate that ranges from a mean monthly temperature of 68 degrees in January to 81 degrees in July, in a land wind-washed with the silken Trades. These hardworking transplanted folk are eager to help their city grow because they know thereby they can continue to prosper in this happy place. The final theoretical population is 560,000 and planners are flexible in building the perfect city.

Education

Well aware are the builders of Lucaya that good educational facilities are of prime importance in attracting and retaining the highly-trained personnel required to man the most desirable type of industry. The community has a kindergarten, a nursery school, three primary schools, two high schools, a secretarial college, ballet and tap-dancing schools and a music school. Education is compulsory in the Bahamas from five through fourteen.

A University of the World

A university of the world may be built in Lucaya. An international university is being studied under the auspices of the 2.6 million member American Lutheran Church, sponsor of 12 independent colleges in the United States. The 300-acre site for the future campus, a grant by the Grand Bahama Development Company, fronts on a 1,400-foot sandy beach on Northwest Providence Channel. Two distinguished Florida architectural firms have the contract to plan the site. A development council has been formed to conduct a campaign to raise $ 10,000,000 to build the university as a part of the feasibility study.

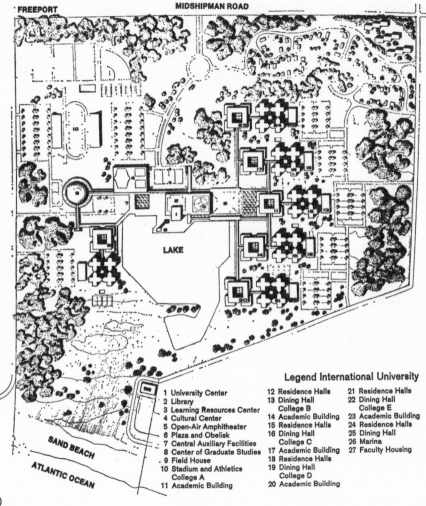

FREEPORT MIDSHIPMAN ROAD

LAKE

SAND BEACH

ATLANTIC OCEAN

Legend International University

1 University Center
2 Library
3 Learning Resources Center
4 Cultural Center
5 Open-Air Amphitheater
6 Plaza and Obelisk
7 Central Auxiliary Facilities
8 Center of Graduate Studies
9 Field House
10 Stadium and Athletics
   College A
11 Academic Building

12 Residence Halls
13 Dining Hall
   College B
14 Academic Building
15 Residence Halls
16 Dining Hall
   College C
17 Academic Building
18 Residence Halls
19 Dining Hall
   College D
20 Academic Building

21 Residence Halls
22 Dining Hall
   College E
23 Academic Building
24 Residence Halls
25 Dining Hall
26 Marina
27 Faculty Housing

Envisaged is an institution of six colleges, one post-graduate, with 5,000 full-time students. The university will be co-educational and residential, open to all academically qualified students without regard to race, nationality or creed. It will not, according to its officials, be a carbon copy of any other university. The curriculum as well as faculty and students will be truly international. It will be free of restrictive tradition so that it can create rather than conform, and it will fit the program to the individual student.

Medical Center

The Colonial Research Institute at Freeport was created by James H. Rand in 1958, with its first and principal goal the building of a comprehensive and up-to-date non-profit medical complex designed to serve the expanding population. The Institute's offices and laboratories are in Freeport, but its interests are widespread and include the financial support of non-profit making activities in the United States and other countries. The facilities include not only an excellent hospital, well-staffed, but also an adjacent modern diagnostic clinic. Among the Institute's other local interests is the operation of a hydroponic vegetable farm where vegetables are grown without the use of modern pesticides. The Institute is also carrying on research for an insecticide that will not be toxic to human beings. Within the complex is the John Harvard Library, ground for which was broken by Dr. Wernher von Braun. Within its ocean-side quadrangle the Institute has also built and furnished residences that are made available free of rent to retiring doctors and scientists of distinction from leading American universities. Important medical services include also the Antoni and Forsyth clinics.

The Bahamas Government and Freeport/Lucaya

The Bahamas have had self-government since January 7, 1964, when a new constitution took effect. Her Majesty the Queen, symbolic head of state, appoints a Governor to represent her in the Bahamas. Constitutionally the powers of the Governor are limited to external affairs, defense, internal security, police and the prerogative of mercy for convicted criminals. Following an election, the Governor is required to name as premier the leader of the party having a majority in the House of Assembly, or of the party in a coalition in which that party is the strongest member.

On January 10, 1967, Lynden Oscar Pindling, a successful lawyer and a friendly fellow called "Ping" by his classmates, became Premier as leader of the Progressive Liberal Party, which had just won the General Election. He was the first Negro and the second native-born Bahamian to become leader of his country. The London-trained lawyer came to Grand Bahama on August 7, 1967, to dedicate a new waterway and to say: "The Government is not about to kill the goose that has laid a golden egg and will continue to lay a golden egg for many years."

To the men and women who had built Freeport-Lucaya he said, "I can see no reason why from this day forth a new and vibrant partnership cannot be forged between those of you who have visited us with your enterprising talents, because it seems to us that we can teach each other."

"We need to learn your enterprising techniques and we need to teach you how not to commit suicide, something we don't believe in. Bahamians believe in living happy, healthy lives until they end somewhere in the nineties, and they are scared to die. You like to make money, so if we can swap one or two ideas and we can learn to make some money, too, while you can learn to live until you are eighty, how much better it will be for us."

The Spirit of Freeport/Lucaya

Freeport/Lucaya is young and exciting. All who work and live there feel a sense of participating in the discovery and growth of the place. There is a community spirit second to none. Individuals, as such, contribute their ideas, good will, financial help, and work; but also the industries, the schools, and the churches work in harmony toward ever-better goals. There is almost no crime, and the few instances of crime are mostly the work of outsiders. The sense of enterprise and personal freedom are un-matched, and many who come to visit decide to stay for a lifetime.

ILLUSTRATIONS

*Activities on the Beautiful Beach
of Lucaya*

All along the southern coast of Lucaya stretches one of the finest white sand beaches of the Bahamas, perfect for all kinds of water sports and seaside activities. Hotels, groups of villas, apartments and homes are located along the beautiful beach. The photograph, showing sailboats and a motor boat with a parachute skier high in the air, was taken on the beach of the Oceanus South Hotel. Note the beautiful clear sea beside the beach.

Harbor at Lucayan Beach Hotel

Lucaya is a paradise for boat owners because of its many beautiful waterways, excellent harbors and marinas. The photograph shows the landing at the Lucayan Beach Hotel and this fine hostelry is visible in the background.

El Casino

In the heart of downtown Freeport, surrounded by a delightful park with foun-tains and pools, is El Casino, designed in the style of a lavish Moorish palace. Within are some of the world's largest and most sumptuous gaming rooms, the romantic candlelit "El Morocco", a dining room with excellent cuisine, and "The Kasbah", a night club with outstanding international revues and shows.

Lucayan Country Club

A mecca for golfers is Freeport/Lucaya. Here you can play 72 holes of golf without once repeating yourself. The golf courses lie between the residential sections of Lucaya and close to downtown Freeport. One of the outstanding golf courses, that of the Lucayan Country Club, is pictured here. Designed by the late Dick Wilson, it is an 18-hole championship course with well-trapped, watered fairways framed by pines and palms and set amid rolling hills and small lakes, with the white sand beach and waterways in the background. Clearly seen in the far upper right in the photograph is the high rise of the Oceanus-South Hotel. A little further to the left, also on the ocean, is the Lucayan Beach Hotel. Just in front of it on Bell Channel Bay is the Harbour House, an apartment building, and to the left the Harbor Inn with a big marina. On a little hill surrounded by the fairways stands the club house and in the foreground are two typical Lucayan homes.

Entrance to International Bazaar
The colorful International Bazaar in downtown Freeport is one of the principal tourist attractions of the resort. In this multi-million-dollar showplace of shops and restaurants you can take a trip around the world, walking from street to street through different countries and cultures. The photograph shows the main gate of the Bazaar, surrounded by a part of the straw market, with an oriental building in the background. With its Spanish, Mexican, Scandinavian, German, French, Indian, Arabian, Chinese, Japanese, South American and English sections, the Bazaar is still growing to the north, and additional attractions can be expected in the near future.

Homes of Lucaya
Lucaya is the residential section of this

great new community. Here are the beautiful modern homes, large and small, each surrounded by a garden with tropical flowers, palms and the Caribbean pine of Grand Bahama. There are also condominiums and many duplexes and apartments for rent. Lucaya is growing fast. It is expertly landscaped with excellent paved roads and many waterways linking the homes of boat-owners to the ocean.

The Home of Wallace Groves
One of the outstanding homes, directly on the ocean, is that of the founder and developer of Freeport/Lucaya, Wallace Groves. It was built in 1962, designed by architect Alfred Browning Parker. The blue-green, ocean-colored roof is made of imported glazed Italian tiles. Outstanding is the spacious living room, scaled for delightful hospitality.

Wallace Groves, Founder and Developer of Freeport, with his Family
This picture, made in his home, shows Virginia-born Wallace Groves, the creator of this new community, with his wife Georgette and three of their five children. In front is Gayle, and behind her Gary and Graham. Absent are the two older children, Jean and Gordon, who spend

their school year in the United States. Their home is designed for easy living and ample entertaining beside the ocean.

The Beautiful Natural Beaches of Lucaya

Looking down from the sixteenth floor of Oceanus-South Hotel, we see the far-reaching white sand beaches of Lucaya and the gentle, crystalline waters that lap the shore. Three little sailboats move slowly in the cooling breeze.

The Sportfishing Fleet of Lucaya

Just between the Lucayan Beach and the Oceanus North Hotels on Bell Channel Bay are the headquarters of fine charter fishing boats. The picture, taken in the evening after the return of the boats, shows a seventy-pound tuna and other prizes in a good day's catch.

The Treasure of Lucaya

By accident in 1965, less than a thousand yards off-shore in front of the hotels in only 20 feet of clear water, four young men – Gary Simmons, Jack Slack, Dick Tindall and Bissell Shaver, operators of the water-skiing and skin-diving school at the Lucayan Beach Hotel – found an early 17th century treasure. To the sur-face they brought silver coins, crude pieces-of-eight, with the insignia of Philip the Fourth of Spain. Thousands of similar coins were found there in a coral en-crusted mass that looked like an ancient anchor, for which Gary Simmons, 25, thought he was diving. The value of the recovered treasure has been set at close to two million dollars. The photograph shows some of the cleaned coins in the hand of a surprised tourist.

Underwater Exploring
in the Clear Ocean around Lucaya

It is a great world for diving, with a reef thriving with colorful underwater life close to the nearby beach. It offers the best of the undersea world, last exciting frontier wilderness on earth. Few waters around the earth can match the clarity, warmth, beauty and abundance of marine life off Lucàya's shores. It is, therefore, natural that the International Under-water Explorers Society, Ltd., has its world headquarters here with the Grand Bahama Underwater Explorers Club, located at the entrance of the Oceanus-North Hotel. There is on hand a profes-sional staff under the leadership of Presi-dent Al Tillman, beautiful club rooms, complete biological and photographic laboratories, a lounge, solarium, saunas, research library, an interesting museum and a 17-foot testing pool. There are daily guided reef trips and down-coast expeditions. The membership fee is nominal and what a pleasure it is to meet here diving enthusiasts from all over the world, such as France's Jacques Cousteau, Dr. Wernher von Braun, Arthur Godfrey, Australia's Ron Taylor, Walter Cronkite, Lloyd Bridges, Coles Phinizy of Sports Illustrated and others, all members of this club.

Hotels of Lucaya
(View over Bell Channel Bay)
Looking from a window of the Harbour House we see four of the luxury hotels of Lucaya on a lagoon across the Bell Channel Bay. From left to right: The Lucayan Beach Hotel, the Oceanus-North, the Oceanus-South and far to the right the Holiday Inn. Their beach front is on the other side, facing the Atlantic Ocean, which is visible in the far background.

Freeport International Jet Airport
Growing with the community is this international airport with one of the best jet runways. It is served by BOAC, Pan American, Eastern, Northeast, Bahamas Airways and Air Canada.

Lucayan Marina, Bell Channel Bay
Grouped round Lucayan Harbor Inn beside Bell Channel Bay, facing the entrance of Lucayan Beach Hotel beyond the bay, is this attractive marina with all of the varied facilities and conveniences that make yachting such an alluring way of life.

Fun around a Swimming Pool
(Holiday Inn)
Every hotel in Freeport/Lucaya has an attractive swimming pool with all the year-around fun, going with it in this idyllic subtropical climate. Holiday Inn is especially popular with young people.

Holiday Inn, Lucaya
It is the largest Holiday Inn in the world, a center of sports and all sorts of other activities for the young and ageless. The photograph shows the splendid wide beach with a group of small sailing catamarans in the foreground. Note the swimming pool to the right, with its tropical outside bar and dance floor for many special parties going on in the afternoons and evenings. The Inn has a big auditorium and numerous meeting rooms.

The Churches of Freeport

The two photographs show two of the churches of Freeport: left, the Anglican Church of Christ the King in the center of town, built by Ray O. Peck, and, right, Our Saviour Lutheran Church, designed in an unusual modern architectural style by Schweizer Associates. The latter is located on East Sunrise Highway, the road to Lucaya. Not far from there is the Roman Catholic Church, Mary Star of the Sea, with an extensive parochial school.

The Famous Deep Water Harbor of Freeport

The Freeport harbor is a major factor in the healthy growth of Freeport/Lucaya and in the continuing upsurge of interest in and economic activity on the island. It is one of the largest and deepest commercial ports in the western hemisphere, with all modern facilities of an international harbor and free port. The photograph shows one of the larger tourist ships, the Franca C, entering the harbor. In the background is a fifty-million dollar cement factory, a subsidiary of U. S. Steel Company. It supplies building material produced from native rock for the fast-growing community.

In a Freeport School

Schools in Freeport are modern in standards, with excellent teachers, principally from Canada, the United States and Great Britain. The children are dressed uniformly to foster equality among them. The picture shows the courtyard of the parochial school Mary Star of the Sea at lunchtime. The classrooms are all on the ground floor of the low buildings visible in the background.

Medical Center

The photograph shows the entrance of the private Doctors Hospital on East Atlantic Drive. It offers complete medical, surgical and psychiatric services. Important also is the Antoni Clinic on East Sunrise Highway, with full dental and medical facilities. Grand Bahama Hospital on East Atlantic Drive is a well-staffed and fully equipped modern hospital.

The Beautiful Seascape of Lucaya

There is plenty of space on the far-sweeping public beaches of Lucaya. The soft sand pillows those who rest on it. Palms and sea grapes border the beach beside the turquoise water, which slopes very gradually to clear depths.

Oriental Building, Freeport
This part of the International Bazaar exemplifies the original idea of building a shopping street with oriental motifs. Out of it developed in 1965–66 the project of bringing in the exotic charms of other places of the globe. Hillard Morris Brown, gifted Hollywood set designer, with Charles Perrin and John Matthams, created the International Bazaar, showpiece of Freeport, and the monumental Japanese Torii gate at its entrance.

Tropical Park in the Heart of Freeport
Typical of Freeport/Lucaya are the wide avenues, the spacious squares and parks, the open beaches and the waterways that evoke a certain good feeling that there is enough space to live, breathe, grow and be happy. There is a beautiful tropical park around a hill just between King's Inn, El Casino and the International Bazaar, visible in the background of the photograph. This is in the busy section of Freeport, an oasis of relaxation and beauty amid fast moving traffic.

John Harvard Library, Freeport
A valued asset of the intellectual and cultural life of the community is an impressive public library, spacious and hospitable. Built by James Rand, it contains several thousand varied books of general interest and a special section of medical literature.

*Hotel Oceanus-South,
the Highest Building in the Bahamas*
Directly on the Lucayan shore rises the Oceanus-South, with its sixteen floors of modern suites and rooms and a unique view from the higher floors over the island and the beach. It was completed late in 1967. The photograph shows in the foreground a small sailing catamaran, very popular with vacationers in exploring the romantic coast of the island.

A Waterfall in the Middle of Town
There is plenty of water in Freeport/Lucaya, and waterways, little lakes and flowing fountains abound. The waterfall pictured in the photograph can be found not far from the entrance of King's Inn.

*Growing Lucaya – New Buildings,
New Roads, New Waterways*
Lucaya is steadily growing, with the extension of new roads and waterways and with new homes and apartment houses rising ever farther to the east and

north. Far to the east, directly beside the beach and the new Grand Lucayan Waterway, is the site of the International University now being planned.

Villas and Homes on the White Beaches
Residents of Lucaya live in new homes, villas and hotels bordering the fine beaches. The photograph shows one such section of the community.

London Double-Deck Buses
for General Transportation
To accent the British influence, typical London double-deck buses have been brought over to serve in the busy regular schedule of transportation and also for sight-seeing.

King's Inn Country Club
King's Inn is the largest hotel in Freeport Lucaya, more than 800 rooms and suites. There is a convention hall with 2500 seats and two championship-caliber 18-hole golf courses with club house and complete facilities including electric carts. The picture was taken at one of the golf courses and shows the clubhouse in the background.

The Indian Section
of the International Bazaar
The originality and charm of the International Bazaar is fostered not only by streets, squares, stores, restaurants and cafés in the styles of many different countries, but also by the people who staff them, nationals of the lands they represent. Here, in the Indian section, East Indians staff the service amid buildings like those of their native country.

El Casino at Night
Night in Freeport is a special experience. Colorful lights play on the exotic buildings, especially El Casino and the International Bazaar. The Bazaar is open until 10 p.m. and some of its cafés and restaurants do not close until later in the night. In El Casino the real life starts at night. Aside from the continental gambling in luxurious surroundings, there are the big shows which start at 10 p.m. in the Kasbah. El Morocco, an outstanding dining room of El Casino, opens at 7 p.m. There is also another elegant casino, the Monte Carlo, at the Lucayan Beach Hotel, and excellent shows at the King's Inn's Camelot Room and Bahamia Club and in the Oceanus-North Hotel.

Panorama-Books by Hans W. Hannau:

each one containing a collection of magnificent color photographs and a dramatic description by this well-known photographer and writer:

ARIZONA · ARUBA · AUSTRIA · BADGASTEIN · BARBADOS · BERMUDA
CALIFORNIA · CALIFORNIA MISSIONS · COLORADO · CAPE COD
COSTA DEL SOL · CURAÇAO · FLORIDA · FREEPORT/LUCAYA · GEORGIA
GUADELOUPE · HAWAII · JAMAICA · LOS ANGELES · MARTINIQUE
NASSAU · NEW JERSEY · NEW ORLEANS
NEW YORK CITY · PALM BEACH · PUERTO RICO · ROMANTIC DANUBE
SAN FRANCISCO · TRINIDAD & TOBAGO · VIRGINIA · VIRGIN ISLANDS
WASHINGTON D.C. · YOSEMITE

Also by the same author, the big volume (9$^1/_2$ x 11$^1/_4$ inches)
ISLANDS OF THE CARIBBEAN
with 48 full page color pictures describing
29 exotic islands of the Caribbean Sea.

PANORAMA-BOOKS

Editor Hans Andermann